W9-BMB-158

MAINE

Copyright © 1991 Steck-Vaughn Company

Copyright © 1986 Raintree Publishers Inc.

All rights reserved. No part of the material protected by this copyright may be reproduced or utilized in any form by any means, electronic or mechanical, including photocopying, record-ing, or by any information storage and retrieval system, without permission in writing from the copyright owner. Requests for permission to make copies of any part of the work should be mailed to: Copyright Permissions, Steck-Vaughn Company, P.O. Box 26015, Austin, TX 78755. Printed in the United States of America.

A Turner Educational Services, Inc. book. Based on the Portrait of America television series created by R.E. (Ted) Turner.

Library of Congress Number: 85-9975

Library of Congress Cataloging in Publication Data

Thompson, Kathleen.
  Maine.

  (Portrait of America)
  "A Turner book."
  Summary: Discusses the history, economy, culture, and future of Maine. Also includes a state chronology, pertinent statistics, and maps.
    1. Maine—Juvenile literature. [1. Maine]
I. Title. II. Series: Thompson, Kathleen.
Portrait of America.
F19.3.T46   1985   974.1   85-9975

ISBN 0-8174-433-8   hardcover library binding

ISBN 0-8114-6785-6   softcover binding

Cover Photo: The Maine Publicity Bureau

    4 5 6 7 8 9 0   96 95 94 93 92 91

★ ★ ★ ★ ★
Portrait of AMERICA

MAINE

Kathleen Thompson

STECK-VAUGHN
C O M P A N Y
A Subsidiary of National Education Corporation

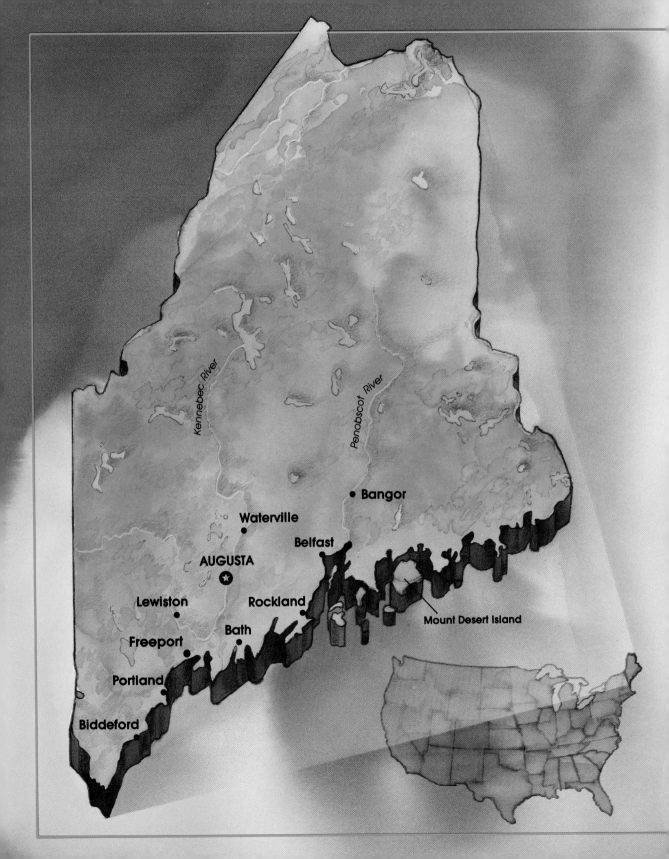

Kennebec River

Penobscot River

● Bangor

Waterville
●

● AUGUSTA

Belfast
●

Lewiston
●

Rockland
●

Mount Desert Island

Bath
●

Freeport
●

Portland
●

Biddeford
●

CONTENTS

Introduction

Maine: the Dawnland.

"(In a small town in Maine) everyone is related to everyone else, almost. They grow up and they stay here. It's not at all unusual to have people who entered the first grade together still working and living in the community. It's news when somebody's away for a week. And it isn't much news in a big city."

Maine: trees, lobsters, tourists, and the land.

"There's so many names put on it. I mean, back to the land and this stuff. It's just a way of life in which you can have the security of being together with so many other forms of life—animal and plant. And the earth."

At the northeast tip of the country, people in Maine see the dawn before anyone else in America. They also see the future coming, like a wave across the sea. And they sit back and watch, deciding which parts of the future seem good, which parts they want to make their own.

The people of Maine value what they have here in the tall trees and the rugged coastline. And they're not about to give it up. They're not turning their backs on high technology, but, like a lot of things in Maine, they're going to take it slowly.

The Maine coast at dawn.

The State That Sees the Sunrise

As long ago as 3000 B.C., Ice Age hunters roamed the land we call Maine. By the time the first Europeans came, Indians of the Algonkian family lived in villages scattered across the area. The Abenaki tribe lived in the west and the Etchemin in the east, divided by the Penobscot River.

The Indians hunted in Maine's forests and gathered wild blueberries. They fished in the rivers and streams. Sometimes they had to move their villages to find food. Sometimes the villages were raided by the Iroquois.

In most parts of the United States, the first explorers were French or Spanish, sometimes English. But in Maine, the first Europeans to set foot on the land were probably from Scandinavia.

Indians fished in streams like this one hundreds of years before the first white settlers arrived in Maine.

Maine State Museum

Vikings had colonized Iceland and Greenland by about A.D. 900, then traveled south and west in about A.D. 1000. So the first European to "discover" this part of the North American continent may well have been Leif Ericson.

In 1968, a Norse penny, made in the time of King Olaf Kyrre (1065-1080), was found at Naskeag Point, near Blue Hill Bay. It may have been brought there by the Vikings.

It's important to remember that a lot of what we think about the early European exploration is just good guessing. Even when the explorers returned with reports of where they had been and what they had seen, they often didn't know themselves exactly where they were. Christopher Columbus died thinking that he'd discovered a new way to the Orient, not a new continent.

But a lot of historians think that the next European to explore Maine was John Cabot (or Giovanni Caboto), an Italian sea captain who was working for England, in 1498. France sent a number of explorers to the area,

A Norse penny (above) was found on the Maine coast in 1968. The penny indicates that Vikings may have landed in Maine in about the year 1000. However, there is still no definite proof that they landed.

including Samuel de Champlain in 1604.

Then, in 1605, George Waymouth explored the coast of Maine. He was sent by two rich Englishmen—Sir Ferdinando Gorges and Sir John Popham—to see if the area was a good one for colonizing. He reported back that it was.

Gorges and Popham decided to put up the money for a group

USDI National Park Service

of colonists to try to settle in the area. At that time, a lot of wealthy men thought of colonizing as a good investment. They provided supplies and ships for the settlers. And then profits from the colony went to them.

In 1607, the settlers landed and set up the Popham Plantation of the Kennebec River. They didn't last very long there. The weather and the Indians drove them away. They returned to England in 1608. But, before they left, they built a ship, the *Virginia*. It was the first boat ever built by English settlers on these shores.

In 1613, Jesuit priests created a mission on Mount Desert Island, off the coast of Maine.

In the early 1620s several settlements were set up in Maine by the English. In 1622, the British Council for New England gave a large piece of land in the area to Ferdinando Gorges—one of the owners of the Popham Plantation—and John Mason. It included land in Maine and New Hampshire. In 1629, the land was divided. Gorges got the Maine area.

After Gorges died in 1647, there were a lot of arguments about who should have the land. Eventually, the Massachusetts Bay Colony paid the Gorges family about $6,000, and Maine became part of Massachusetts.

Below is a painting of Modockawando, chief of the Abenaki tribe from 1669 to 1698.

Collection of the Bangor Historical Society

Collection of the Maine Historical Society

This hemp purse was woven in about 1800 by Mollyocket, an Anasagunticook Indian, who was the most highly rated weaver of her era.

From that time until the early 1800s, Maine was governed from Boston. But France hadn't given up hope of winning a claim to the area. From the late 1600s to the middle 1700s, France fought to get control of the area. Because the French had always been careful to make friends with the Indians, they were able to get the Indians to fight with them against the English. The French and Indian Wars ended in 1763 with the Treaty of Paris. France gave up its claims to Maine and most of the rest of North America.

But then Great Britain made a big mistake. They were beginning to worry that the American colonies were getting too independent. So they decided to rule the colonies with a firmer hand. They started limiting trade, telling the colonists who they could sell to and buy from. They also started putting higher and higher taxes on the supplies colonists bought from Europe.

One of the things they taxed was tea. In 1774, a group of colonists in Maine burned a supply of tea that had come from Britain and was stored at York. During the Revolutionary War that was to follow, hundreds of Maine men went to fight. At least a thousand of them were killed. The British burned the town of Falmouth, which was Maine's major city. It is now Portland.

The first battle at sea during the War took place off the coast

Maine Maritime Museum

The two insets against the modern sailing ship are nineteenth-century photographs of shipbuilding at Bath.

of Maine. The Americans won. Maine patriots captured the British ship *Margaretta.*

When the war was over, Massachusetts gave land in Maine as a reward to its soldiers. The colony also sold a lot of Maine land to other settlers. The population of Maine grew.

But as the settlers chopped down trees in the huge forests and began to build some of the world's finest ships, they also began to grumble. Boston was a long way away. And they paid an awful lot of taxes to Massachusetts. And they didn't seem to get that much in return. After the War of 1812, the people of

Maine decided they weren't getting much protection from the government in Boston, either. In 1819, Maine voters decided to separate from the state of Massachusetts. In 1820, they entered the Union as the twenty-third state.

Maine was admitted to the Union at the same time as Missouri, part of the Missouri Compromise. At the time, the South wanted to make sure that the slave states did not get outnumbered and the North felt the same about the free states. So Maine entered the Union as a free state and Missouri as a slave state and the numbers remained even.

In 1834, the Temperance Movement started in Maine. Many people felt that alcohol was causing a lot of social problems. Women were often the leaders in this movement because they and their children were victims of violence from drunken husbands. In 1846, Maine passed a law that outlawed making and selling alcoholic beverages. In 1851, another law, with better enforcement written into it, was passed and stayed in effect until 1934.

Maine Maritime Museum

Portrait of America

The other political movement that was strong in Maine at this time was the antislavery movement. When the Civil War began, Maine sent 72,000 men to fight. The man who was Lincoln's vice-president during the war, Hannibal Hamlin, was from Maine.

After the war, different kinds of manufacturing became important in Maine. Two of the biggest were the cloth and leather industries. During the late 1800s and the early 1900s, there were fewer and fewer small farms.

Large farms were started for growing potatoes and for raising cattle and poultry. Some of the cloth factories left the state, but the paper industry grew.

During the 1940s a woman named Margaret Chase Smith was elected to the House of Representatives from the state of Maine. Later she was elected to the Senate and served until 1973. Margaret Chase Smith was the first woman ever elected to both houses of the U.S. Congress. She was a New England Republi-

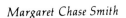

Margaret Chase Smith

Margaret Chase Smith Library Center

can, with a sense of integrity. She spoke out strongly during the McCarthy era, in her Declaration of Conscience Speech.

During World War II, Maine's shipbuilders again became important to the nation. The shipyards in Bath and South Portland made ships for combat and for carrying supplies.

In 1955, Maine created a Department of Economic Development. Along with a number of community groups, the department brought new industries into Maine. The paper companies grew by leaps and bounds. And then something happened that is typical of the state. People began to get seriously worried about the land. And the water. And the air.

With all the new industry, the rivers, for example, began to be too dirty to enjoy. The state passed laws requiring that the rivers be cleaned up. Industry, especially the paper industry, cooperated so well that by 1983, 90 percent of the rivers met standards for water quality. And it didn't stop there.

Maine politicians in Washington battled for a Clean Water Act for the entire country. Rivers all over the United States are being brought back to life because of the people of Maine.

In the late 1970s, an amazing thing happened. The Passamaquoddy and Penobscot Indians went to court, claiming that they owned two thirds of the land in Maine. They based their claim on treaties made between the Indians and the federal government. And they had a very good case. In 1980, the United States government agreed to pay the tribes $81.5 million for the land.

The other important thing that has happened (or hasn't happened) in Maine in the last few decades is that a lot of things haven't changed. While there are a lot of people in the state who have very little money, there are virtually no urban slums. A lot of the social problems that cursed the rest of the country in the 1960s and 1970s left Maine almost untouched.

Perhaps an old Mainer put it best when he said, "I ain't agin' the world goin' modren. I'm jest waitin' a spell to see where she's gonna end up."

The Acadians

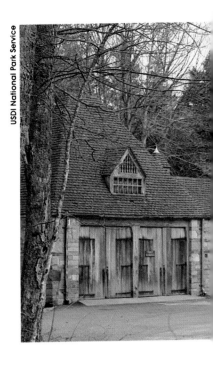

"I think the Acadian culture means to me being Roman Catholic, having close family ties, having strict discipline at home—I still believe in discipline— and being happy with what I am, what I am and what the family is. That's being Acadian to me."

Much of the early history of Canada was a struggle between France and Great Britain. People from both countries had settled on the land. During these struggles, a large group of French settlers was driven from its home, Acadia. Families were separated. All that the people had built was destroyed.

Some of the people of Acadia traveled to Louisiana to be near other French settlers. They became the Cajuns. Another group set up new homes in northern Maine. Many of them, like the family of Real Hebert, still speak French and follow the customs of their ancestors.

The Hebert family came to this land in 1632. They trace their ancestors back for twelve generations. They are happy living and working with others from the same tradition.

"I think it's a friendship that we all have, all together. We know almost everybody around us, and we feel close to everybody. That's very important to me."

The Acadians here in Maine keep alive old customs of language, music, and of food. One Acadian dish, a pot en pot, requires two days to prepare. It uses seven different kinds of meat.

The children of the Hebert family learn French at home. They use both French and English in their schools. And yet, as close as they are to their French Canadian neighbors, the Heberts are Americans. And when they had a family reunion recently,

At the right is an Acadian schoolchild. Above is a Tudor gatehouse at Mount Desert Island in Acadia National Park.

people came from seven Canadian provinces, but they also came from twenty-five states of the United States.

"By being Acadian in this day and age here in the United States, we're not saying we want to go back to the past. Of course not. It's just that if there is no past, there is no present and there is no future."

USDI National Park Service

Life on the Edge of the Forest and the Sea

Take all five of the other New England states and put them together. You'll have just a little more than the area of Maine alone. But a full 85 percent of that Maine land is covered with trees. Half of Maine's territory is not politically organized. That means that nobody much lives there.

The other thing to remember about Maine is that it's cold. It doesn't have quite the spectacular blizzards of North Dakota, where the wind rushes over flat, treeless land. But the winters are quite hard enough, thank you. And the weather affects more than just noses peeking out over mufflers and toes, which can be warmed at a fire.

Most of the people in Maine make their living, directly or indirectly, from the land.

The Maine coast in summer.

First—always first—there are the trees.

The major area of Maine manufacturing is paper products, made from the trees of Maine's forests. The paper industry produces cardboard, paper bags, and pulp, as well as paper. Almost 25 percent of the value of goods produced by manufacturing comes from the paper industry.

Maine is a consistent leader in the nation's supply of paper products. But the paper companies here are leaders in another area as well. In the past ten years, the paper industry has invested over $150 million in air and water treatment to improve the quality of the environment. And they're leaders in energy conservation.

On the average, U.S. paper companies generate about 47 percent of their own energy requirements by burning bark, waste wood and so forth. Some of Maine's paper plants generate up to 90 percent. That leaves more energy from other sources available for the people of the state.

The third largest area of manufacturing also depends on the trees. (We'll get back to the

Fraser Inc.

Portrait of America

second largest in a minute.) The sawmills of Maine produce about a billion board feet of lumber every year. Maine also produces more toothpicks than any other state. And Maine factories also

Two photographs of paper manufacturing (left and above, left) are shown against a background of a logging operation.

Fraser Inc.

Bernard Carpenter, L.L. Bean

make wooden boxes, canoes, clothespins, fences, furniture, ice cream sticks, matches, skis, splints, and toys. They make lobster traps for their own lobster fishers. And a lot of trees are sold to be decorated and stand over a pile of presents at Christmas.

The second largest area of Maine manufacturing is leather goods. L.L. Bean, one of the country's largest shoemakers, is here in Maine. They sell shoes and other outdoor gear through a mail-order catalog.

Above is a shoemaker at L.L. Bean, Inc. Below is a group of pines that will go into people's homes at Christmastime.

Next, in manufacturing, is food processing. Wild blueberries are harvested and quick-frozen in southern Maine. Russet potatoes, grown in the north, are made into frozen french fries. Chicken is processed in Maine and so are sardines. Maine packs more sardines than any other state.

Maine factories pack a lot of the fish caught on the state's shores, including shellfish such as clams, lobsters, and shrimp. They also pack a variety of foods that sound like the menu for the first Thanksgiving—squash, beans, pumpkins, cucumbers, and apple juice.

The textile—cloth-making—industry is important in Maine. It was once much larger than it is, but some factories moved to the South, where labor was cheaper. There are cotton and woolen mills in various parts of the state.

And now we come back to the trees. There is another industry that started in Maine because of the trees. Shipbuilding. Today, the huge ships that slide out of the shipyards at Bath are made from steel. But the shipbuilding industry continues to provide jobs for thousands of Mainers.

Altogether, manufacturing accounts for 82 percent of the value of goods produced in Maine. But the second biggest money-maker produces no goods at all.

Tourists come into Maine by the millions. Summer is the big time. They come to play in the sun, sail, go white-water boating, eat lobster. But in the winter they come, too. They ski, ride snowmobiles, buy their Christmas presents at L.L. Bean.

National Christmas Tree Association, Inc.

Maine Department of Agriculture

Eggs account for the largest part of Maine's farm income.

And it's not that the people of Maine don't want the tourists around. They do. Most of them. But there's a delicate balance to be kept here. If too many tourists come in and cause too many changes, then none of the tourists will want to be here. And neither will the Mainers.

There's farming in Maine, too. It accounts for about 14 percent of the value of goods produced here.

The biggest part of the farm income comes from livestock, and the biggest part of the livestock is, not chickens, but eggs.

In this case, we know which come first, at least in terms of value. But Maine farmers also produce about 70 million broiler chickens a year.

Idaho and Washington grow more potatoes than Maine, but they're the only states that do. About 90 percent of the Maine potato crop is grown in Aroostook County in the northern part of Maine. But then, Aroostook County is the largest county east of the Mississippi.

The coast of Maine is a paradise for the fishing industry. Maine leads the country in lob-

Maine Department of Agriculture

Maine is the third-largest potato producer in the United States.

sters. It's one of the leaders in all kinds of shellfish. And there are cod, flounder, ocean perch, pollock and sea herring in the nets, too.

Fishing is a traditional job for Mainers. So are many of the other ways that the people of this state make a living. They excel at things that require skill, hard work, and a respect for the land and the sea. One of the reasons they're so good at these jobs is that they love them. That's an important thing to remember when you look at the economy of Maine.

When cost of living is taken into account, Maine is fiftieth among the states in per capita income. But a lot of people in this state have chosen life styles that don't require a lot of money. They grow their own food and build their own houses, fish in the ocean and hunt in the forests. They don't fit into easy ways of measuring wealth.

To go back to the words of the legendary Maine oldtimer, "Yep, we have less of everything here. Less crime, less divorce, less children gone bad, less pollution, and less cutthroat competition."

Collection of the Maine Historical Society

Portrait of America

The Ships and the Boats of Bath

"And it's hey, ho, roll and go
Round Cape Horn to San Francisco.
Chantyman, sing, boys pull on the line
And we're back in record time."

It was the early days of a new land, not yet a nation. The trees came crashing down in the vast Maine forests. And the ships grew, towering over the bay, in the town of Bath. Maine shipbuilders made the ships that carried the riches of the land over the world.

"At Bath up in Maine, they built many
tall ships.
They were pared out and planked and
then launched down the slips.
The strength of a nation was built on
the pine
Of the mast trees that harnessed the
wind."

Today, the ships are made of steel. And the Bath Iron Works is the largest industrial employer in the state. Its five thousand employees have a rare reputation for making quality ships.

Down the coast a few hundred

Below is a present-day worker at the Bath Iron Works. At the left is a nineteenth-century photograph of a ship being built at the Works.

yards, ten students at a time are working on a different scale. They are working as apprentices to learn the craft of building wooden boats. They receive no wages and they pay no tuition. The boats they build are sold to pay for the school. And they are learning a special skill.

"I do think that there are a lot of craftsmen with a tremendous amount of valuable experience that's going to be lost if it's not passed on. Taking time to build something is great. There's a certain joy in having a physical product resulting from your work."

The students come from all over. Some left high-paying jobs in offices in the city to learn about another kind of life. They stay here for two years. Of course it's not your usual vocational training program.

"Doing something that you love, that's why we're doing this kind of thing, you know. I mean, it's not like you're going into engineering. There's not a sure job out there for you."

In fact, for most of the students, there may be no job at all. They may never be able to make a living making boats. But there's something about boats. And there's something about the sea. On land, the wilderness can be tamed. And more and more, it's being tamed. But the sea will always be as wild as it was a thousand years ago. The same

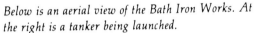
Below is an aerial view of the Bath Iron Works. At the right is a tanker being launched.

Bath Iron Works Corporation

winds will blow and the same waves rise up against the sky. And there will always be people who look to the sea for the adventure they can't find on land.

Love of the sea and pride in a hard job well done—it's an almost unbeatable combination.

"You know, I came here to learn wooden boats. I'd like to make my own wooden boat someday. And my big goal in life is to sail across the Atlantic solo in the boat that I've made. Boy, that's a big undertaking. But I know I'll do it."

Lambs, Looms, and Low Tech

"Well, I think I was a romantic. I think I was an early day hippie. I was looking to get away from the establishment. I had a dream that was a very personal dream. I didn't expect to do anything earth shaking. I just am a sheep freak. I like sheep, and I feel that they're absolutely magnificent beasts. The animal with the golden hoof."

Bob and Sue Dunlap came to Maine from Chicago thirty years ago. They were drawn to a way of life that seemed slower and closer to the land than their life in the city. They weren't sure what they were going to do or what they were going to find.

"We just came here in an old pickup truck, camped in a tent and finally found this land. And we had an old clunker of a loom. We didn't have any money. When you start out a winter not knowing how you're going to get through it, it can be less than fun. And then of course, you get the 'My, you are brave.' We weren't brave. We didn't have any better sense. And we loved what we were doing."

They found the land and began raising their sheep. And then they had an idea.

"Actually, Sue was the first one to come up with the idea of making a scarf from the backs of our own woolly sheep. And oddly enough, it worked."

It certainly did. Today, the Dunlaps have ten weavers and finishers working for them. They use looms that are run by motors, but the weaving is all done by hand. The fibers that are used are all natural.

The Dunlaps train the weav-

ers who work for them, and each piece of work that leaves their workshop has a tag with the weaver's name on it. The weav-

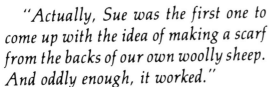

Rosalie Wetmore

ers get fan mail from all over the country. Their scarves and accessories have appeared in the pages of *Vogue* magazine. They're carried in fine shops all over the Northeast.

"We're making things for people by hand so that they've got something that is a little singular. It should reflect the fact that there's somebody who has thought about it, given it some care. That's part of the reason for concentrating on the quality is that in the midst of all the mass production, somebody's still there doing things by hand because they care about it."

The Dunlap Weavers are successful. But for Bob and Sue, there is something else that is even more important. They found the life they were looking for when they came to Maine thirty years ago.

"You can't really go around saying, 'I'm the luckiest man in the world,' can you? But I feel that way. And it's true. I mean, who else could do almost exactly what he planned and wanted to do?"

Portrait of America

Bob Dunlap and one of the Dunlap Weavers are shown against the background of sheep, from which they get their wool.

The Maine Publicity Bureau

Art in the Towns and the Forests

"*T*he *poet must, from time to time, travel the logger's path, the Indian's trail, to drink something new at the fountain of the Muses far in the recesses of the Wildnerness.*"

The great American author Henry David Thoreau wrote these words 130 years ago. He came to Maine and wrote a book called *The Maine Woods*. Writers have been coming here to write ever since.

Actually, some writers were in Maine before Thoreau. Harriet Beecher Stowe wrote the classic antislavery novel *Uncle Tom's Cabin* in Maine. She also wrote a book set in Maine, *The Pearl of Orr's Island*.

And many writers were born in Maine. The great popular poet Henry Wadsworth Longfellow was born in Maine. One

Moosehead Lake in Greenville

Photos, Collection of the Maine Historical Society

Henry Wadsworth Longfellow.   *Harriet Beecher Stowe.*

of his most famous poems, *Evangeline,* was written about the Acadians. Sarah Orne Jewett, one of the first important women novelists in American literature, was born and raised in Maine and wrote about life in New England.

Another famous woman in American literature, Edna St. Vincent Millay, was a native Mainer. Her book, *The Harp-Weaver and Other Poems,* won the Pulitzer Prize in 1923. Another Pulitzer Prize winner was Edwin Arlington Robinson, whose *Collected Poems* were honored in 1921.

Nathaniel Hawthorne wrote in Maine. More recently, E.B. White came to live and write in Maine. He set his famous children's book, *Charlotte's Web,* on a Maine farm. The remarkable pig with the spider for a friend was exhibited at the Blue Hills Fair.

Writers have not been the only artists drawn to the beauty of Maine. Winslow Homer, one of America's greatest artists, painted the sea and the sailors of

Above is a group of people playing at a music festival.

Maine. The Wyeths, father and son, have both come to Maine to paint.

A world away, but still in Maine, there is Douglas Trumbell, who designed special effects for films like "2001" and "Star Trek." He has set up a studio in Maine.

It would be impossible to name all the artists and crafts people who have lived and worked in Maine. The atmosphere is perfect for any kind of creativity.

There is peace, beauty, and solitude. And in the cities, there is a high level of cultural activity. There are music and dance groups, some of whom travel around the state, performing in small towns. One small town held an animated film festival, drawing people from all over the state.

And these days, people all over the world are hearing music that comes straight from the heart of Maine.

The Maine Publicity Bureau

Maine Music Produces a Classic

"We really feel that we have the best of both worlds. As performing musicians, we tour the world. We get to spend our time in the big cities. We get to travel. And yet we get to live in a state that has natural beauty, that has a little bit slower pace of life."

The Portland String Quartet has just recorded their seventh album. They are respected in the world of classical music far beyond the borders of Maine. They are also a valued part of their community and their state.

"People expect the audiences here to be very conservative, but I've found them to be very openminded as far as what we play. The typical, stereotyped Mainer will tell you what he thinks. But they're willing to listen."

The Portland String Quartet is part of a tradition of fine music in Maine. But still, when they came here, the musicians worked hard to make a place for their music.

"Fifteen years ago, there was not a quartet here. The artistic climate was very weak. Then we came in and began going to small towns and playing literally hundreds of concerts."

The quartet still travels around the small towns of Maine. They lecture and give concerts around the state and around the country. They are considered international experts in coaching young orchestras. And they feel that living in Maine has helped their music.

"It's very delightful. It doesn't crowd in on you. And frankly, creatively speaking, you feel a lot freer."

When the quartet talks about performing in Maine, you hear a theme that echoes through much of what people say about the state.

"It's a much less anonymous feeling than you get living in an enormous population center. And it's a very friendly feeling. It's a very human feeling."

A member of the Portland String Quartet.

Portrait of America

The Maine Publicity Bureau

Choosing a Future

There's nothing standing between Maine and what most people call progress . . . except Maine itself. Maine is a very attractive state with a lot of natural resources. And as soon as they decide exactly what they want to do with the future, you can be sure they'll do it. But in Maine, people look before they leap.

At a time when energy is one of the first things that new industry looks for, Maine has the greatest hydroelectric power in New England. And there is more power in the waters of Maine just waiting to be harnessed. But the governor recently announced limits on dam building in order to preserve the rivers for their beauty and for recreational uses like white-water boating. In Maine, people seem to believe

White-water rafting on the Penobscot River.

Below is a lobster trap and at the right is the L.L. Bean store in Freeport.

Bernard Carpenter, L.L. Bean

Portrait of America

that you can have things both ways if you're careful.

The tourist industry is booming. But Maine is not the kind of place that builds huge theme parks, casinos, and fancy resort hotels. That's not the kind of life the Mainers live, and they're wise enough to realize that Maine offers something unique to its visitors. You can find theme parks anywhere. Only in Maine can you enjoy the roadside lobster stands and small country fairs and rough outdoors that make Maine the place it is.

One of Maine's business success stories is L.L. Bean. For over seventy years they have made and sold all kinds of outdoor gear. They had the kind of reputation that Maine craftsmen and manufacturers so often do. They sold quality products, made well and made to last. About ten years ago, they began advertising and selling by mail nationwide. Today, their sales have reached a quarter of a billion dollars a year. Two million people a year come to the L.L. Bean retail store in Freeport.

Now Freeport is faced with a problem. Hundreds of other companies want to open stores to take advantage of such a large group of possible customers. And Freeport isn't sure it wants them. It likes being the kind of small town it has always been.

This is a classic Maine situation. The possibilities are there. But the people aren't just going to jump at them. They're going to think about them, talk about them, and then make a choice.

Bernard Carpenter, L.L. Bean

Important Historical Events in Maine

1000 Leif Ericson probably lands on the Maine coast at about this date.

1498 John Cabot, an Italian sea captain sailing for England, probably explored the Maine coast.

1524-
1604 Giovanni da Verrazano, Pierre du Guast, Sieur de Monts, and Samuel de Champlain explore Maine.

1607 The first permanent English settlement in Maine, Popham Colony, is established near the mouth of the Kennebec River.

1620s England establishes many permanent settlements.

1622 England grants Ferdinando Gorges and John Mason much of the land of Maine and New Hampshire.

1641 Gorgeana—today called York—becomes the first chartered English city.

1677 Massachusetts buys Maine from the family of Ferdinando Gorges.

1689-
1763 The French and Indian Wars take place in Maine and various other parts of New England.

1763 The Treaty of Paris is signed, and France gives up its claims to almost all of North America.

1774 Maine citizens burn a supply of British tea at York. The action is called the York Tea Party, after the Boston Tea Party of the year before.

1775 Americans and English fight the first naval battle of the Revolutionary War off the coast of Maine in June.

1820 Maine votes for separation from Massachusetts and becomes the 23rd state on March 15. The capital is Portland, and William King is the governor. Maine, with Missouri, is a part of the Missouri Compromise.

1842 The signing of the Webster-Ashburton Treaty ends disputes over the Maine-Canada border.

1851 Maine makes it illegal to manufacture or sell alcoholic beverages in the state.

1940-
1973 Margaret Chase Smith becomes the first woman to be elected to both houses of Congress. She served in the House from 1940 to 1949 and in the Senate from 1949 to 1973.

1958 Edmund S. Muskie becomes the first Democrat to be elected to the U.S. Senate from Maine. He is the vice-presidential candidate in 1968.

1969 Maine passes a law taxing both personal and corporate incomes.

Maine Almanac

Nickname. The Pine Tree State.

Capital. Augusta.

State Bird. Chickadee.

State Flower. White Pine Cone and tassel.

State Tree. White Pine.

State Motto. *Dirigo.* (I direct.)

State Song. State of Maine Song.

State Abbreviations. Me. (traditional); ME (postal).

Statehood. March 15, 1820, the 23rd state.

Government. Congress: U.S. senators, 2; U.S. representatives, 2. **State Legislature;** senators, 33; representatives, 151. **Counties:** 16.

Area: 33,215 sq. mi. (86,026 sq. km.), 39th in size among the states.

Greatest Distances. north/south, 332 mi. (534 km.); east/west, 207 mi. (333 km.). **Coastline:** 228 mi. (367 km.).

Elevation. Highest: Mount Katahdin, 5,268 ft. (1,606 m). **Lowest:** sea level, along the Atlantic Ocean.

Population. 1980 Census: 1,124,660 (13% increase over 1970), 38th among the states. **Density:** 34 persons per sq. mi. (13 persons per sq. km.). **Distribution:** 52% rural, 48% urban. **1970 Census:** 993,722.

Economy. Agriculture: eggs, milk, broiler chickens, beef cattle, hogs, sheep, lambs, turkeys, potatoes, oats, beans, peas, sugar beets. **Fishing Industry:** lobsters, clams, perch, scallops, herring, shrimp. **Manufacturing:** paper and wood products, textiles, leather, processed foods, electric and electronic equipment, automotive equipment, shipbuilding. **Mining:** sand and gravel, granite, crushed stone, limestone, clay, copper, zinc, gemstones.

Places to Visit

Acadia National Park in southeastern Maine.

Black Mansion in Ellsworth.

Burnham Tavern in Machias.

Fort Western in Augusta.

Old Gaol Museum in York.

Penobscot Marine Museum in Searsport.

Portland Head Light, near Portland.

Tate House in Portland.

Wadsworth-Longfellow House in Portland.

White Mountain National Forest in southwestern Maine.

Annual Events

Downeast Tennis Classic in Portland (May).

Clam Festival in Yarmouth (July).

Maine Broiler Festival in Belfast (July).

Windjammer Days at Boothbay Harbor (July).

Blueberry Festival in Union (August).

Maine Seafoods Festival in Rockland (August).

State Fair in Lewiston (September).

Maine Counties

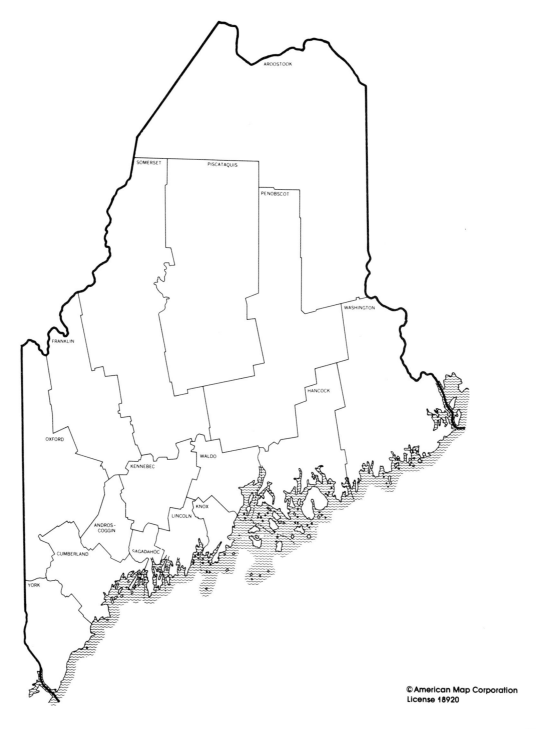

AROOSTOOK

SOMERSET

PISCATAQUIS

PENOBSCOT

FRANKLIN

WASHINGTON

HANCOCK

OXFORD

KENNEBEC

WALDO

KNOX

LINCOLN

ANDROS-COGGIN

CUMBERLAND

SAGADAHOC

YORK

© American Map Corporation
License 18920

INDEX